God bless you!

Margaret

SOOTHE YOUR SOUL

*Meditations to Help You through
Life's Painful Moments*

REV. MARGARET VREDEVELD

A DIVISION OF WRITER'S DIGEST

Unless otherwise noted, Bible quotations are from the
New Revised Standard Version (NRSV)

Unless otherwise noted, hymns are public domain hymns.

Used by permission:
Spirit, Spirit of Gentleness: Words and Music Copyright ©
1978 by James K. Manley. All Rights Reserved.
Hymn of Promise: Words & Music: Natalie Sleeth © 1986 Hope Publishing
Company, Carol Stream, IL 60188. All Rights Reserved.

Used by permission:
Eight graphics by Meliah V. Mead
Abbott Press books may be ordered through booksellers or by contacting:

Abbott Press
1663 Liberty Drive
Bloomington, IN 47403
www.abbottpress.com
Phone: 1-866-697-5310

ISBN: 978-1-4582-1215-3 (sc)
ISBN: 978-1-4582-1214-6 (hc)
ISBN: 978-1-4582-1213-9 (e)

Library of Congress Control Number: 2013918241

Printed in the United States of America.

Abbott Press rev. date: 10/23/2013

In loving memory of

Sheri Joy Vredeveld April 4, 1973 - April 11, 2001

Table of Contents

INDEX OF MEDITATIONS FOR PAINFUL MOMENTS

Acknowledgements

Words can't truly convey my deep gratitude to the people who have walked with me on this journey of the soul, but I DO say, "Thanks!"

Especially to my family: Ron, Julie, Scott, Cindy, Sheri, Meliah, Kaya and Lucille. You haven't always liked what I had to say, but you always affirmed my right to say it and you honored my unique expression. I know it was sometimes annoying that I had a song for every comment, but—still—you sang along with me. I'll always remember telling you stories with and without lyrics! What a gift to me!

To my former parishioners at Clare Congregational United Church of Christ: Thanks! In becoming your teacher and pastor you pastored and taught me.

To my friends and colleagues at Immanuel Lutheran Church: Thanks! You helped me find my voice. Special thanks to Marilyn Zorn for reading my manuscript and offering suggestions. Thanks to Dan and Jennifer Digman who helped me brave the world of publishing.

To my former voice students: Thanks! In teaching you the art of singing, you taught me the art of listening.

To James K. Manley: Thanks for inspiring and encouraging me!

To a very special artist, Meliah Mead: Thanks for the drawings! They are such a wonderful reflection of what our family has shared over the years.

To the Staff at Abbott Press: Thanks for all your support.

Foreword

These meditations chart the course of a mother and pastor through a wilderness of loss and sorrow toward a spiritual clearing of hope and renewal.

I have heard Rev. Margaret singing her sermons and read her articles in the local newspaper and always have admired her grace and humanity.

This book will allow a wider group of readers to share her thoughts and experiences and her ever-maturing faith.

Marilyn Zorn

Margaret has always shared her creative genius with her family. We enjoyed her cooking, listened to her stories, proudly wore the clothes she sewed, and enjoyed the beauty she created in our home.

We enjoyed her gift of music whenever we traveled by car—she had a song for every occasion. She blessed our lives as she sang in churches and later when we sang with her.

While she was studying in seminary and serving as a pastor, we enjoyed watching her share her creative writing and creative presentations with other people. Her sermons inspired us and many others—deepening their spirituality through reflection on the stories of God's people and the simple events of everyday life.

We are thankful that now she will share her stories, insights, and reflections with a broader audience. We know that her creative reflections on life in this book will provide for you, as they have for us, renewed hope, deeper peace, and concern for God's people and creation.

Ron, Julie, Scott, Cindy, Meliah and Kaya

Preface

In April, 2001, my youngest daughter Sheri Joy died at age twenty-eight of ovarian cancer. She had survived since her diagnosis in July, 1996 and we had been very hopeful that a relapse in September, 2000 was just that—a relapse. She asked me to be her spiritual guide as she began to realize she was dying. Every night I would pray the Psalms with her and practice Reiki (healing hands) on her body. My husband and I embraced her at the end and I remember saying, "I was there for her first breath and her last."

During this time I was pastoring my church and I became painfully aware of the suffering people experienced during all of life's transitions. In serving my people during this difficult time my sermons and meditations began to reflect the fact that I knew what it was like to walk through the valley of the shadow of death with my own child.

People began to affirm that my words and voice were soothing to the soul. When I decided that in retirement I would make the effort to reach a wider audience through meditations, I volunteered to write on a regular basis for the religion page of a local newspaper. My twin began to say, "You should write a book. I guarantee you will have readers."

Now—after five years—I have found the courage to do so.

Rev. Margaret Vredeveld, M div

A Song of the Soul

by Margaret Vredeveld

*See what great love God has given us that we
should be called children of God.*
I John 3:1

*I see myself walking on the shore of Lake Michigan—
Waves gently roll in—wetting the sand—
Making a ruffle pattern on the shore.
The sun is at my back and the breeze seems to gently push me north.
I see the little girl playing in the sand—
Her curly blond hair shining in the sun.
She squats as only a small child can. She is two years old.
She looks up at me as my shadow crosses her place in the sand.
What a beautiful smile she has! Baby teeth like pearls.
She watches me as I pass—unafraid of me.
I am the child.
She is my innocence.
My inner light.
My soul.
I am—at center—a child of God.
No thing and no one can take that away from me.*

Trust God and Give God Thanks

Boredom

TRUST GOD AND GIVE GOD THANKS

I stand at the kitchen window looking out on yet another bleak, rainy day and I find myself lamenting the flu that has kept me grounded too many days. It's bad enough to GET the flu—why does it have to linger so long? And why does my husband have to be sick too? Two grumpy people in one house is one grumpy person too many! I find myself wondering—is it just me or does the world seem darker to everyone when he or she feels sick? I watch the news and it feels like war and hatred and violence hover over my soul like a dark cloud. A story about "balloon boy" makes me weep for exploited children everywhere. I ask God, "Why do the wicked prosper?"

As I ponder I find myself singing (silently, since my voice is gone!) the prayer by Sy Miller and Bill Jackson: *"Let there be peace on earth and let it begin with me."* I breathe as deeply as flu allows and let myself imagine a world where all people—no matter what their age—know they are at center children of God. I imagine that quiet trust radiating from every individual until it becomes a force that overcomes war and hatred and violence. It is as if a light comes on in my soul and the dark world is infused with hope.

In my mind I see the prophet Jeremiah in ancient Israel—afflicted, afraid and alone. I hear his lament and recognize in it the healing and hope that arise even during his time of overwhelming anguish. The healing and hope that spring from his trust that he is at center a child of God:

> *The thought of my affliction and homelessness*
> *Is wormwood and gall!*
> *My soul continually thinks of it and is bowed down within me.*
> *But this I call to mind, and therefore I have hope:*
> *The steadfast love of God never ceases.*
> *God's mercies never come to an end;*
> *They are new every morning;*
> *Great is your trustworthiness.*
> *"God is my portion," says my soul,*
> *"Therefore I will hope in God."*
>
> Lamentations 3:10-24

I raise my eyes to the window and see not just the dreariness of the day but color. Gold. Red. The startling whiteness of my neighbor's house. And I pray for the people I can't visit because I am sick. I pray for exploited children. I pray for the wounds of the people of the world. I pray for peace.

Go ahead. Lament! Tell God how unfair it is that you are sick. Tell God how you feel. Pour out your troubles and worries. Recall God's love for you in the past. Project into the future the light of the hope that God will continue to renew and guide you.

No matter what your situation, trust God. And give God thanks for the gift of life.

A Light upon My Path

Christmas

A LIGHT UPON MY PATH

I sit in my living room next to the advent wreath mesmerized by the light from the candles—lights symbolizing hope, peace, joy, and love. In my mind I see of the light of the star that guided the magi to Bethlehem. What extravagant gifts the magi carried! Frankincense, myrhh and gold. Gifts fit for a king. I wonder what Mary and Joseph did with all that gold! My mind wanders to the gifts we give and receive. Some are extravagant—some not. Some fit—some don't. And we must wait in irritatingly long lines to return or exchange them. Then I think of the gifts God has given us. Extravagant and fitting gifts—spiritual gifts: hope, peace, joy and love.

I focus on the light of the candle symbolizing hope—not a feeling but an awareness—a light shining in the darkness reminding us that we are at center children of God. And I remember the stirring words of Jeremiah in Lamentations 3. Words from a soul despised and rejected:

The thought of my affliction and homelessness is wormwood and gall! My soul continually thinks of it and is bowed down within me. But this I call to mind, and therefore I have hope: The steadfast love of the Lord never ceases. God's mercies never come to an end; they are new every morning; great is your faithfulness. "God is my portion," says my soul, "therefore I will hope in God."

And I pray for us as we enter a new year that we might hold

within us God's gift of hope as a light upon our path and so be hopeful people.

I focus now on the light of the candle symbolizing peace—not a feeling but an awareness—a light shining in the darkness reminding us that we are at center children of God. And I remember the comforting words of Jesus in John 14. Words to a people afraid of the future:

Do not let your hearts be troubled. Trust in God, trust also in me. In my Father's house there are many rooms. If it were not so, would I have told you that I go to prepare a place for you? And if I go I will come again and will take you to myself, so that where I am, there you may be also. . . . Peace I leave with you; my peace I give to you. I do not give to you as the world gives. Do not let your hearts be troubled, and do not let them be afraid.

And I pray for us as we enter a new year that we might hold within us God's gift of peace as a light upon our path and so be peaceful people.

I focus now on the light of the candle symbolizing joy—not a feeling but an awareness—a light shining in the darkness reminding us that we are at center children of God. And I remember the comforting words of Isaiah 35. Words to a people devastated by war and driven from their homes:

The wilderness and the dry land shall be glad; the desert shall rejoice and blossom . . . . A high way shall be there, and it shall be called the Holy Way; . . . the ransomed of the Lord shall return, and come to Zion with singing. Everlasting joy shall be upon their heads; they shall obtain joy and gladness, and sorrow and sighing shall flee away.

And I pray for us as we enter a new year that we might hold within us God's gift of joy as a light upon our path and so be joyful people.

I focus now on the light of the candle symbolizing love—not a feeling but an awareness—a light shining in the darkness reminding us that we are at center children of God. And I remember words from

Jesus in John 3. Words telling Nicodemus we are born not just of our human parents but of God.

For God so loved the cosmos that God sent God's only begotten Son into the cosmos that everyone who believes in him may not perish but have everlasting life. Indeed, God sent not the Son into the cosmos to condemn the cosmos, but in order that the cosmos might be saved through him.

And I pray for us as we enter a new year that we might hold within us God's gift of love as a light upon our path and so be people full of love.

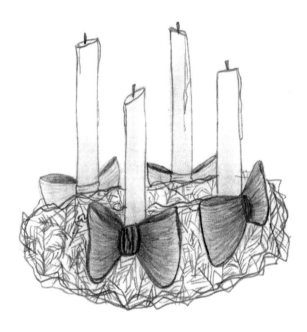

Now, as I focus on the collective lights of the candles, I think again of the magi and their extravagant gifts—gifts fit for a king. And I thank God for God's extravagant and fitting gifts to us—hope, peace, joy and love—not feelings but awarenesses—lights shining in the darkness reminding us that we are at center children of God.

Now may the God of hope fill you with all joy and peace in believing, so that you may abound in hope by the power of the Holy Spirit. Romans 15:13

The War of the Squirrels

Conflict

THE WAR OF THE SQUIRRELS

I sit in my kitchen mesmerized by the squirrel show at my neighbor's bird feeder. Two squirrels devise a way to scatter seed on the ground and feed companionably for about one minute. Now one begins to chase the other—around and around they go! Now one escapes into the tree circling quietly and waiting for its chance to pounce. The other carefully creeps out of the woods and begins to feed. Now the tree squirrel attacks and—around and around they go again. This goes on for about thirty minutes and I begin to wonder how much energy they are using in this war for seeds. It seems to me there is enough seed for both if they would just continue to feed companionably and not spend so much energy chasing each other.

Now I notice the news is on and turn my attention to the TV. So much squabbling over territory and power! It seems to me just another version of the war of the squirrels. Everyone wants to be top squirrel. If only all the energy expended in war could be redirected into co-existence! If only everyone lived by the Golden Rule:

In everything do to others what you would have them do to you.
Matt. 7:12

Now a memory surfaces: I hear my three children arguing in another room. Someone says, "I'm telling mom!" The teller leads the way to my door eager to justify her position before her sisters can speak. "Mom, they're not letting me have my turn!" The rebuttal: "It's not her turn! It's my turn!" "No—it's my turn!" Then the pushing and shoving begins. I stand between them and ask each one, "Do you like to be shoved? Then don't shove your sisters." Then the latent preacher in me says,

> "Remember the Golden Rule—in everything do to
> others what you WANT them to do to you—
> not what they DID to you."

But many seem to operate by this perversion of the Golden Rule: Do to others—in an even more vengeful way—what they did to you. Others make up their own perversion of the Golden Rule. I once knew a man who told people he operated by his own golden rule: He who has the gold rules. Though—it seems to me—it was his gold that ruled him. I'm pretty sure his golden rule did not help him when death came calling. Wealth may appear to make a person top squirrel on earth, but is irrelevant in eternity.

Now—just as I begin to feel depressed about humanity—the news moves to a segment called "Making a Difference." I watch people apply energy to the global issue of clean drinking water. I watch people apply energy to the rebuilding of Joplin, Missouri. I watch people apply energy to helping the victims of the raging forest fires in Colorado. And I find my trust in God's grace and in humanity revived.

I pray now for the global community: That we may learn to harness our energy and expend it in ways that help people and that honor God's image in all people. That we truly treat other people the way we want to be treated.

Imagine such a world! Do your part by using the Golden Rule as your guide in everyday life.

Take a Lesson from
the Sunflower

Confusion

TAKE A LESSON FROM THE SUNFLOWER

God is my light and my salvation;
Whom shall I fear?

Psalm 27:1

Have you ever noticed how sunflowers seem to turn their faces towards the sun? It's as if—on some deep level—they know the source of their life.

It makes we wonder how our lives would change if we could remember—on some deep level—that God is the source of our life. God is our light. We instinctively want to turn our faces to God, but the cares of life weigh us down and make us turn away. As we turn away the road before us grows dark and we wonder whether God has turned away from us. Feeling disconnected from our source of life, we look for security in other things—things that draw life from us.

When I feel as if I'm floundering in the dark, I often find myself singing a gospel song by Helen H. Lemmel:

O soul, are you weary and troubled?
No light in the darkness you see?
There's light for a look at the Savior,
And life more abundant and free!

Turn your eyes upon Jesus,
Look full in His wonderful face,
And the things of earth will grow strangely dim,
In the light of His glory and grace.

I know it is hard to face the wearying and troubling issues of life. We feel sometimes as if we do not have enough energy to turn to the light. And—sometimes—the light seems to reveal too much. We see what lurks in the dark corners of our minds and it frightens us. Then the word of God comes to us:

God is my light and my salvation; whom shall I fear:
God is the stronghold of my life; of whom shall I be afraid?
. . . for God will hide me in God's shelter in the day of trouble.

. . . Wait for God, be strong;
Let your heart take courage,
Wait for God! [Psalm 27]

Take a lesson from the sunflower. Let your instinctive yearning for God turn you to the light. Let the light of the world shine upon you. Strengthen you. Comfort you. Sustain you.

More than the Sand

Death of a Loved One

MORE THAN THE SAND

On Wednesday, May 16 (my birthday) I walk out of our trailer which is just up the hill from a small County Park in Michigan. I can hear the sound of the waves and feel the wind—I head back inside for my flannel shirt. Now I make my way behind the other trailers to the road and catch my first view of Lake Michigan. I walk down the hill, across the parking lot, towards the boardwalk overlooking the beach. I won't walk the beach today—I don't want to get sand-blasted. There are no people on the beach and I walk the boardwalk quietly hoping to see a great blue heron. No—not today. Only once in thirty-six plus years of coming to this spot have we ever seen a heron on the shore of Lake Michigan—eleven years ago on Memorial weekend.

I REMEMBER it as if it were yesterday! It was a day much like this—windy, chilly—the beach-goers had given up and headed home early. My husband and I walked hand-in-hand towards the boardwalk carrying within us our broken hearts. It had been just a month and a half since our daughter's death and it seemed like we were just going through the motions. Suddenly my husband put up his arm to stop me. Slowly he pointed to the beach and there it was. A great blue heron standing where the creek empties into the lake. As we watched, the great bird rose on its wings—must have been a six-foot wingspan—and flew north along the shore, over the dunes and into the trees. Our spirits rose as if on the wings of that great bird!

21

I tuck the memory away and gaze at the lake and SUDDENLY it seems as if I am there at Creation: I see the mountains rise out of the heart of the sea. I watch as plant and animal life is created. Now I watch God gather the dust of the earth and create humankind in God's image and breathe into their nostrils the breath of life.

I feel again the wind on my face and realize it is 2012 and I am on the boardwalk. I BREATHE deeply and my soul sings quietly:

You moved on the waters, you called to the deep, then you coaxed up the mountains from the valleys of sleep. And over the eons you called to each thing, "Awake from your slumbers and rise on your wings." Spirit, Spirit of gentleness, blow through the wilderness calling and free. Spirit, Spirit of restlessness, stir me from placidness, wind, wind on the sea.

Now I gaze at the blowing sand and it seems like a vast wilderness. I REMEMBER all the times in my life when I felt lost in the wilderness of my mind because something was ending and I couldn't see what was beginning. I or someone I love had been dreadfully sick. I had been grieving the loss of a loved one through death or divorce. I had lost a job. I was being bullied or abused. Times when I wondered whether my life was of any more value than a grain of sand.

And SUDDENLY it seems as if I am there in the wilderness with the children of Israel some 3,200 years ago. There are hundreds of people. All they've known is slavery—and now they make their way through the wilderness to the Promised Land. I watch as Moses comes down the mountain with the Ten Commandments on tablets of stone. I watch as they build a container—the Ark of the Covenant—in which they place reminders of God's promises: The commandments, a portion of manna and Aaron's rod which has budded. I watch as they cross the Jordan River and march around the city of Jericho. I see the walls fall and watch as the territory is divided among the 12 clans. I watch as the Judges lead the people—Samson, Deborah, Gideon. Now Samuel, who is both a judge and a priest, meets the sons of Jesse bypassing each warrior brothers and choosing the boy, David, a shepherd, poet and musician.

I watch David begin to build the temple and place within it the

Ark of the Covenant. I see him in a room in Jerusalem dictating a new song to his scribe:

Oh God, you have searched me and known me. You know when I sit down and when I rise up; you discern my thoughts from far away. You search out my path and my lying down, and are acquainted with all my ways. Even before a word is on my tongue, O God, you know it completely. You hem me in, behind and before, and lay your hand upon me. Such knowledge is too wonderful for me; it is so high that I cannot attain it. Where can I go from your spirit? Or where can I flee from your presence? If I ascend to heaven, you are there; if I make my bed in Sheol, you are there. If I take the wings of the morning and settle at the farthest limits of the sea, even there your hand shall lead me, and your right hand shall hold me fast . . . . For it was you who formed my inward parts; you knit me together in my mother's womb. I praise you, for I am fearfully and wonderfully made. Wonderful are your works; that I know very well. My frame was not hidden from you, when I was being made in secret, intricately woven in the depths of the earth. Your eyes beheld my unformed substance. I your book were written all the days that were formed for me, when none of them as yet existed. How weighty to me are your thoughts, O God! How vast is the sum of them! I try to count them—they are more that the sand; I come to the end—I am still with you. [Psalm 139]

Now I feel the wind on my face and realize it is 2012 and I am on the boardwalk gazing at the blowing sand. I BREATHE deeply and my soul sings quietly:

* *You swept thru the desert, you stung with the sand, and you goaded your people with a law and a land; When they were confounded by their idols and lies, then you spoke through your prophets to open their eyes. Spirit, Spirit of gentleness, blow through the wilderness, calling and free, Spirit, Spirit of restlessness, stir me from placidness, wind, wind on the sea.*

Now the sun breaks thru the clouds and I feel the warmth on my face. I gaze at the beach and REMEMBER family times. Three little girls playing in the sand and water become teenagers and then women in the blink of an eye.

And SUDDENLY it seems as if I am there with Jesus's ancestor

David 3,000 years ago. I watch Solomon complete the temple and am dismayed to see his sons turn on each other and begin a civil war dividing the kingdom into Israel in the north and Judah in the south. Now the Assyrians capture the north and soon the Babylonians take the south destroying the temple and ravaging Jerusalem. The Ark of the Covenant disappears. I hear the prophets talk of a new king who will be born of the line of David. I see the Persians defeat the Babylonians and watch young Esther become queen and put a stop to a plot to kill all Jews. Now people return to Jerusalem and rebuild. I watch as one power after another takes control of Jerusalem. Now Roman peace ushers in the right time for the king born of David's line. I see the star over Bethlehem. I hear a newborn cry and the lullaby of parents. I watch Jesus grow and minister. Now I see the three crosses on the hill and hear the weeping of the women. I see Mary Magdalene at the tomb—astonished at Jesus's resurrection. Now—fifty days later (during the feast of Pentecost) I see the disciples in a room, hear the wind, see the flames. I watch Peter stand and say,

These are not drunk, as you suppose. . . . No, this is what was spoken through the prophet Joel: In the last days it will be, God declares, that I will pour out my Spirit upon all flesh, and your sons and your daughters shall prophesy, and your young shall see visions, and your old shall dream dreams. Even upon my slaves, both men and women, In those days I will pour out my Spirit; and they shall prophesy." (Acts 2)

Now I feel the wind and the sun and look out over the beach. I BREATHE deeply and my soul sings quietly:

You sang in a stable, you cried from a hill, then you whispered in silence when the whole world was still; and down in the city you called once again, when you blew through your people on the rush of the wind. Spirit, Spirit of gentleness, blow through the wilderness, calling and free, Spirit, Spirit of restlessness, stir me from placidness, wind, wind on the sea.

Now my eyes are drawn to the top of the dune we call "Sugar Bowl." And I REMEMBER sitting at the top with my first-born daughter eleven years ago on Memorial Sunday. We didn't need words. We just sat shoulder to shoulder. My thoughts were full of doubt—how can there be enough room in heaven for all our loved ones who have died!? I looked down at the beach and noticed how small the people seemed from our perspective on the dune. The dog that had snapped at my grandkids looked no bigger than an ant! I remember getting the goose bumps that come with enlightenment: *Eye has not seen, nor ear heard, nor human imagination envisioned what God has prepared for us.*

Now a gust of wind brings me back to 2012 and SUDDENLY it seems as if the veil between time and eternity is lifted. Loved ones who have died are with me. They are not sick or old and feeble. They are at peace and joyful. I see my heroes of the faith—Miriam and Moses, Mary and Jesus, Sojourner Truth and Harriet Tubman. Martin Luther and Dr. Martin Luther King. There is no sense of time—just eternity. I see others and realize they are the souls of those as yet unborn. A great cloud of witnesses.

Now I gaze as far as my eyes can see—down the shoreline and to the horizon. The dunes above me. The sky and clouds. I BREATHE deeply and my soul sings quietly:

You call from tomorrow, you break ancient schemes, from the bondage of sorrow the captives dream dreams; our women see visions, our men clear their eyes. With bold new decisions your people arise. Spirit, Spirit of gentleness, blow through the wilderness, calling and free, Spirit, Spirit of restlessness, stir me from placidness, wind, wind on the sea.

Now the wind picks up, the sun disappears into the clouds and I feel cold. Wrapping my flannel shirt around me I head for the warmth of my trailer. It is so much easier to walk with the wind at my back! I ask God, "What do you want me to tell your people on Pentecost?" and it seems as if God is saying, "Tell the people what you have seen today. Tell them that the same Spirit who was there at creation is with them and within them now and for all eternity."

So I tell you: the same Spirit who was there at creation is with you and within you now and for all eternity. This is the message of Pentecost. Thanks be to God.

Spirit, Spirit of Gentleness: Words and Music Copyright © 1978 by James K. Manley. All rights reserved. Used by permission.

Ode to My Easter Child

Easter

ODE TO MY EASTER CHILD

I sit in my comfy chair in my living room warmed by the sun streaming in through the windows and marveling at the way the sunlight enhances the colors in the room. I take in the sight of my piano, family pictures, plants and mementos.

I begin to think about the date this meditation will be printed and I realize April 7 is Holy Saturday—the day before Easter. And in my mind I see myself on Holy Saturday eleven years ago. Family members crowd my living room waiting till 3:45 p.m. when we open the front door and begin the sad procession to Cherry Grove Cemetery. As ready as anyone ever is for the burial ritual, we walk bathed in sunlight and I notice daffodils and crocuses are in bloom— so beautiful! With a heavy heart made lighter by the loved ones who walk with me, I make my way to my daughter's final resting place. There—on Holy Saturday, 2001 we sing *Amazing Grace: Through many dangers, toils and snares I have already come; tis grace has brought me safe thus far, and grace will lead me home.*

I think of that day eleven years ago and feel what Mary Magdalene must have felt on that first Holy Saturday some two-thousand years ago. So dreadfully tired. So sad. So confused. So angry. I watch her as she prepares her ointments for the burial ritual. Unable to sleep she rises early on Sunday morning, gathers what she needs and makes her way to what she thinks is the final resting place of her teacher, her friend, her companion.

I see her weeping at the discovery that the tomb is empty—who would add insult to injury by stealing his body?! Now she becomes aware that someone is standing by her side asking, "Why are you weeping?" And she—looking at him through the veil of her tears and supposing him to be the gardener—says, "Sir, if you have carried him away, tell me where you have laid him, and I will take him away." [John 20]

I hear the stranger's voice—full of compassion
and love—utter one word: "Mary."
I feel her absolute astonishment as she recognizes
Jesus and says, "Dear teacher."
They walk and talk together. And, oh how amazing it all is!
Caught up in the joy of this re-union I find myself
singing the C. Austin Miles hymn:

I come to the garden alone,
While the dew is still on the roses;
And the voice I hear, falling on my ear,
The Son of God discloses.
And he walks with me, and he talks with me,
And he tells me I am his own;
And the joy we share as we tarry there,
None other has ever known.

I close my eyes and meditate upon all the ways God walks and talks with us—bringing light and life into our darkest, saddest moments.

Through the touch of a hand, a kind word or a gift of food.

Through the sight of a butterfly—a symbol of resurrection.

Through the warmth of the sun and the color of the flowers.

Through scripture, poem or song.

On this Holy Saturday open your eyes to see God walking with you. Open your ears to hear God talking with you—saying to you, "You are my own."

See What Love the Father Has Given Us

Father's Day

SEE WHAT LOVE THE FATHER HAS GIVEN US

As I think about God as "Father" the image comes to mind of my husband bending over the sickbed of our daughter Sheri tenderly wiping her face, listening to her, speaking softly to her, and cradling her in her moment of need.

Such gentleness.

Such compassion.

Such love.

In that image I see God having compassion for us. Caring about our suffering. Whispering words of comfort. Listening to us. Cradling us. And I know we are loved by God in times of joy and in times of sorrow. We are in God's hands. It puts me in mind of the words of the Psalmist: *As a father and mother have compassion for their children, so does God have compassion for those who respect God.* Psalm 103:13 (New Century Hymnal)

But I know that many of you have no positive images of your father. And my heart goes out to you. Perhaps no earthly father cradled you. Or was gentle with you. Or listened to you. Or had compassion for you. And the image of "Father" God is foreign or even frightening to you.

If so, take courage! Think of someone in your life who has shown compassion to you in your moment of need. Compassion is borne of God; therefore, that person—male or female—who had compassion for you embodies God's love for you. That person is your spiritual mother and father. Hold the image of that act of compassion in mind and you will know what it is to experience God's compassion for you.

And remember—<u>you</u> are a child of God. Whenever <u>you</u> have compassion for people in their moment of need, <u>you</u> embody the love of God. <u>You</u> carry on the legacy of the heavenly Father and become spiritual mother and father to souls in need.

> *See what great love the Father has given us*
> *that we should be called children of God;*
> *and that is what we are.*

> I John 3:1

Hand In Hand
(A meditation for spousal vows)

Fear of Commitment

HAND IN HAND

We tend to think of love as a feeling. Because of this, we begin to worry—when we are feeling sad, afraid or angry or when our emotions are numbed by life's events—that love has died. But the love to which we commit today is much more than a feeling. It is a philosophy—a way of being derived from the specific Greek word *agape*. To love in the *agape* sense is to value, respect and deeply appreciate.

In I John 4: 7-12 the writer puts it this way:

Beloved, let us love one another—[let us value, respect and deeply appreciate one another]—because love is from God; everyone who loves is born of God and knows God. Whoever does not love does not know God, for God is love. God's love was revealed among us in this way: God sent the only son into the world so that we might live through the son. In this is love: Not that we loved God but that God loved us and sent the son to be the atoning sacrifice for our sins. Beloved, since God loved us so much, we ought to love one another. No one has ever seen God; if we love one another—[if we value, respect and deeply appreciate one another]—God lives in us and God's love is made complete in us.

I could say more about the word "love" but instead—I want you to pay attention for a moment to the fact that you are standing here hand in hand. And let this hand-in-hand-ness be an abiding metaphor for the deep love to which you commit today.

You stand here hand in hand. No one forced you to come to

this moment. You have chosen to join hands because you love each other—you value, respect and deeply appreciate each other.

You stand here hand in hand. Remember this moment when you are angry and tempted to hurt each other. In remembering this moment you show that you love each other—you value, respect and deeply each other.

You stand here hand in hand. Remember this moment when you are apart—as you will be at times. See that you remain trustworthy in every way. Faithful to each other in every way. In being trustworthy you show that you love each other—you value, respect and deeply appreciate each other.

You stand here hand in hand. And I assure you that hand in hand you will have more strength when life hurts you—as it will. And hand in hand you will have more joy when life blesses you—as it will.

You stand here hand in hand in the presence of friends and family who love you—who value, respect and deeply appreciate you. Who stand ready to lend you a helping hand.

You stand here hand in hand in this holy place—

This holy place with its stained glass windows reminding us of God's rainbow promise.

This holy place with its cross reminding us that by dying Christ defeated death.

This holy place with its arched ceiling reminding us that by rising Christ opened to us the gates of eternal life.

Just as this holy place encircles us—so do God's hands encircle us. We are children of God and God loves us—God values, respects and deeply appreciates us. God never forgets us. God speaks through the prophet Isaiah:

Can a woman forget her nursing child,
or show no compassion for the child of her womb?
Even these may forget,
Yet I will not forget you.
See, I have inscribed you on the palms of my hands. (Isaiah 49:15-16)

Beloved, since God so loves us—so values, respects and deeply appreciates us—we ought to love one another. No one has ever seen God; if we love one another—if we value, respect and deeply appreciate one another, God lives in us and God's love is made complete in us. Thanks be to God.

Sticks and Stones

Gossip

STICKS AND STONES

As I meditate upon the power of words a memory surfaces: I am shopping at a grocery store when I hear a loud, scolding voice. I turn and notice a seventyish woman shaking her finger at her husband—at least I assume it is her husband—and berating him. He shrinks away from the tongue-lashing and I sense how demeaned and disheartened he feels.

The memory still haunts me and—when I ask myself why—I find myself chanting, "Sticks and stones can break my bones but words can never hurt me." As a child I would chant this through my tears whenever someone said something that really hurt. Now I know the truth. Sticks and stones can break my bones but words can break my heart. And not just actual written or spoken words. A gesture, a tone of voice, body language—with or without words—can break your heart.

Gossiping words. Who among you has not walked into a room towards a group of people who suddenly shush each other and look away or even disband leaving you to wonder whether something hurtful is being said about you. What it is you may never know because it is being said behind your back. But you worry that it might become fodder for phone or internet chatter. Gossip is a form of character assassination. Gossiping words can break your heart.

Euphemistic words. Words prettied up to cover up an ugly truth.

Words like "friendly" fire. If you know someone killed by "friendly" fire your heart has been broken not just by the loss of your loved one but by the attempt on someone's part to justify the loss with pretty words. Euphemistic words are—in essence—lies. Euphemistic words can break your heart.

Abusive words. Words that demean and belittle—perhaps disguised as "teasing" or "kidding." My heart has been broken many times by hurtful words spoken in anger and then dismissed with a laugh and a mean-spirited taunt, "I was just teasing! Wow! You're so sensitive! Grow a thicker skin!" It is as if the one using hurtful words is deflecting responsibility for his or her meanness by casting blame on you. This tactic seems to pull the rug out from under you leaving you lying on the floor confused—unsure that you can trust yourself and your sense of what is true. You lose confidence in yourself. Verbal abuse is a form of identity theft. Abusive words can certainly break your heart.

You and I have all had words used against us—many times. Sometimes in the heat of the moment but also—many times—in a purposeful manner calculated to derail us. Oh yes! Gossiping, euphemistic, and abusive words can break your heart.

It is certainly something to consider in this electronic age when it is so easy to take pot shots at people with words. Perhaps we would all be more careful of the words we use if we heeded the words of Jesus in Matthew 12:36:

I tell you, on the day of judgment you will have to give an account for every careless word you utter; for by your words you will be justified and by your words you will be condemned.

All of us have hurt people by what we have said or implied. Aware of this, my personal motto has become: "It is better to say too little than too much." Take time to think about what you are going to say before you say it.

Take time TODAY to say something kind to someone.

Arthritis of the Soul

Grief

ARTHRITIS OF THE SOUL

It seems to me that grief is a chronic condition like arthritis. Arthritis of the soul—so to speak. The pain is always there. Sometimes it is manageable and sometimes it flares up—often when least expected. Sensory experiences—sights, sounds and smells—evoke memories and we find ourselves reliving painful moments.

But while we usually have a plan of action to manage physical arthritis pain, we leave ourselves vulnerable to the pain of grief. I suggest a plan of action for arthritis of the soul: Awareness, acceptance and action. Become aware of how you feel when pain has been triggered. Accept and feel the feelings. Take purposeful action. When flashbacks bushwhack us we tend to react by trying to run away. While we can't control being bushwhacked, we can learn to temper our reactions by taking purposeful action. Purposeful action is preferable to reaction. Sometimes the best purposeful action is inaction—sitting still and letting ourselves feel what we are feeling. Memorials on anniversaries, birthdays and holidays are purposeful actions that can—over time—ease the intensity of "flare-up" moments.

The memorial events broadcast on Sunday, September 11, 2011 are a great example of purposeful action. The sight of people kneeling, weeping and touching the names of their loved ones. The sound of the waterfalls in the background. These sensory images allow all of us to remember our loved ones, to weep for them, and to remember the promise of rebirth. As my husband and I watched the televised memorial on that day we talked quietly through our tears of what we were doing on September 11, 2001 which came exactly five months after the death of our daughter Sheri on April 11, 2001. We talked about how difficult the 11th of each month was. As time passed I learned to be gentle with myself on the 11th of each month. I learned to pause and allow myself to feel and lament. It seems to me that the memorials on 9-11-2011 were healing for all of us because they allowed us to feel and lament personally and nationally. It calls to mind the lament of the prophet Jeremiah. Experiencing his own arthritis of the soul he cries out:

The thought of my affliction and homelessness is wormwood and gall. My soul continually thinks of it and is bowed down within me. But this I call to mind, and therefore I have hope: The steadfast love of the Lord never ceases. God's mercies never come to an end; they are new every morning; great is your faithfulness. "God is my portion," says my soul, "therefore I will hope in God." (Lamentations 3: 19-24)

Awareness, acceptance and action. I began to learn this life lesson one morning about three months after our daughter's death when I awoke feeling rested and happy until I remembered. Desolation enveloped me. I acknowledged the pain of my broken heart. And, attempting to ease the pain, I prayed Psalm 23 and kept repeating "Yea, though I walk through the valley of the shadow of death, I will fear no evil for thy rod and thy staff—they comfort me." I began to relax and doze as I meditated and suddenly I heard the words, "You must go through the valley—and I will go with you." From that moment on instead of trying to run away from the valley I started to purposefully walk through it to the light on the other side.

Our lives are full of both joyful and sorrowful memories. To run away from the sorrowful is to run away from the totality of who we are. It's my new "normal"—this awareness of tragedy and acceptance of it as part of my life. I can never again be who I was before my heart was broken by grief. I do suffer from arthritis of the soul, but I am not diminished by the chronic nature of my pain because I know who walks with me through the valley. And I walk purposefully—grateful for the gift of life.

The Tree That Survived

Hard Times

THE TREE THAT SURVIVED

Come with me on a road trip! It's Tuesday, February 5 and our daughter in Boston phones: "Hey we're supposed to get two-three feet of snow starting on Friday." We panic because we were planning to drive Friday and Saturday. "It's possible my Sunday concert will be cancelled. I can get you into the dress rehearsal on Thursday night. What do you think?" First we panic. Then my husband and I turn on the Weather channel. We notice a big storm is predicted for Michigan on Thursday. So we decide we need to leave the next day and we begin to throw stuff together for the journey. We change our motel reservations from Friday to Wednesday and text our daughter to let her know our plans.

Next morning we hit the road bringing with us far more than we would have had we not been rushed. I even pack my sermon readings for March 3 just in case. I notice that the lessons are invitations to come to the water and be fed by God. The gospel lesson is the parable of the fig tree and I remember how a gardener promised to nurture the tree. It's a beautiful drive—pristine snow from Tuesday's storm, sunshine. The trees sparkle with hoarfrost. Hoping to avoid lake effect snow we take a southern route through Pennsylvania calling our daughter from Wilkes-barre at night. "Well," she says, "now there is supposed to be a blizzard! Jim Cantore is heading to Boston—if that tells you anything! Please stop tomorrow to pick up some groceries because after work on Thursday the stores in Boston will be crazy."

Again on Thursday it is a beautiful drive through the mountains—The trees glisten with their snow frosting. I say to my husband, "It's so beautiful—it's hard to imagine there is a blizzard coming." But we stop for groceries just in case. Thursday night we follow our daughter to a sheltered parking lot where we park our car for the weekend. On we go to her rehearsal—Mahler's *Song of the Earth*. With her voice she paints a tone picture of the joys and sorrows of life and the hope of eternity.

Friday everything is shutting down in Boston—we drive to a favorite breakfast place as the snow starts to fall. From there our daughter takes us to a pharmacy near her condo; we walk to her house from there while she drives HER car to the sheltered lot and takes the bus home. We hunker down. And the wind shrieks like a banshee! And it snows! Boy, does it snow! Saturday morning we look out on a world of white. I notice that the trees are bending from the weight of the wind and snow—sideways snow. I marvel at the ability of the trees to survive.

Saturday and Sunday pass and we are grateful for electricity! We can cook and watch TV. Use all our devices. We hear Boston will be shut down for snow removal on Monday and Tuesday—the days we had hoped to drive home. We check The Weather Channel looking for the optimal travel day—looks like Ash Wednesday is the only day when there is no snow predicted for Boston, Albany, Buffalo, Cleveland or Clare. We decide to leave Boston at 5 a.m. Ash Wednesday and drive straight home—no matter how long it takes.

I'm the first driver but we switch every 1½ to 2 hours. I notice the trees again—lifting their bare wintertime branches to the sky. Some straight up. Some gnarly and bent. Some are fallen. The white skin of the birches catches the filtered sunlight. Again I marvel at ability of the trees to survive the winter. Driving around Buffalo we breathe a sigh of relief—We both remember being caught in a Blizzard in Buffalo In 2000! Not an experience to be repeated! We stop at the westernmost oasis of the NY Thruway and grab a free sample of cinnabon.

Now it is my turn to drive. I'm so sleepy that I decide to ask my husband to take over but he is doing his best imitation of a bobble-head doll. I now regret that cinnabon I ate—sugar coma. Trying to keep alert I quietly sing along with my James Taylor Cd—*Winter, spring, summer or fall*—and do the eye popping exercise and the shake-of-the head exercise. And still hubby bobs away. Now I can see Lake Erie with its masses of ice near the shore. Lots of vineyards. I say a silent prayer for the Great Lakes States—that we won't have an early Spring and the trees will blossom and bear fruit. And still hubby bobs away. Now I do mental exercises. I ponder the word snow. I ask myself—if c-o-w is pronounced cuhoo and n-o-w is pronounced nuhoo—why is s-n-o-w pronounced snoh? Shouldn't it be pronounced snuhoo? I let my mind wander and ponder the parable of the fig tree marvelling at the grace of the caregiver who doesn't give up on the struggling tree. Now Ken Medema's Tree Song comes to mind and I consider the wintertime verse as the start of the children's sermon. God cares for the trees—and for us.

Now—while I am truly grumpy and irritable—my husband wakes up all cheerful and talkative and we reach our gas station in Ohio. Yay! Now he can drive and I can sleep. I close my eyes— but, alas, now I am wide awake—my mind caught in its stream of consciousness pondering. I think again of the fig tree and trees that survive the winter. I think of the Church Year. Epiphany and Lent.

In Epiphany we celebrate God's abundance.

In Lent we confess our emptiness and claim God's compassion.

The Question is—how do we experience God's abundance in times of emptiness—times when we feel cut down by life. When we are sick and weak. When we are grieving. When we are poor. When we despair. When we are ashamed. Then I remember that God's love is universal and God's grace surrounds us all of the time—not just when we feel blessed, but also when we feel bereft. I recall the astonishing words of Isaiah 55:

Ho!—EVERYONE who thirsts, come to the waters;

And you that <u>have no money</u>, come, buy and eat!

Come, buy wine and milk without money and without price.

Now I feel the car slowing and give up the pretense of sleep. I open my eyes. It's Cleveland where we lived with our three little girls before moving to Mt. Pleasant. We were happy there. Now we reach the Ohio Turnpike and—stopping at the first oasis—get coffee and hit the road again. I drive asking Ron to pop in a CD— in case he nods off again. I sip my coffee determined to make it last the entire time I drive. I continue to ponder the fig tree and the wintertime tree, abundance and emptiness. I sing *Blest Be the Tie that Binds* along with my brothers:

> *Before our Father's throne*
> *we pour our ardent prayers.*
> *Our bears, our hopes, our aims are one—*
> *Our comforts and our cares*
>
> *We share our mutual woes,*
> *Our mutual burdens bear—*
> *And often for each other flows*
> *The sympathizing tear.*

I realize the song has answered my question: How do we experience God's abundance in times when we are empty—when we feel cut down? Through song, scripture and people—children of God. People are our kindly gardeners. Some of you have tended me in my emptiness. I'll never forget: It was 1981. I was struggling to adapt to life in Mt. P. I hadn't wanted to leave Cleveland State University where I was a respected commuting music student with a scholarship. I hadn't wanted to uproot our kids from school. Here I felt betrayed by some University staff who told me scholarships were reserved for younger students. I was 35. Here I was increasingly fed up with the way women were cut down in the church of my birth. Finally, bullied by a new minister, I fell apart. I was ready to give up on church. But I visited Immanuel where communion and the readings for the day lifted me up. Together we chanted what would become my life song—Psalm 116:

I love God because God has heard my voice and my supplication.
Because God listened to me, therefore I will call upon God all my life.
The snares of death encompassed me; the pangs of Sheol laid hold on me;
I suffered distress and anguish,
Then I called on the name of God; "O God, I pray, save my life!"
Gracious is God, and righteous; our God is merciful.
God protects the simple; when I was brought low, God saved me.
Return, O my soul, to your rest,
For the Lord has dealt bountifully with you,
For you have delivered my soul from death,
My eyes from tears, My feet from stumbling.
I walk before the Lord in the land of the living.
I kept my faith, even when I said, "I am greatly afflicted";
I said in my consternation, "Everyone is a liar."
What shall I return to God for all God's bounty to me:
I will lift up the cup of salvation and call on the name of God,
I will pay my vows to God in the presence of all God's people.
Precious in the sight of God is the death of God's faithful ones.
O God, I am your servant . . . . You have set me free.

I thought I might regain my confidence as a singer by becoming a Cantor. It was dreadful. My knees knocked, my hands shook, my book bounced, my tongue stuck to the roof of my mouth. I went home and cried. "I guess I am just not cut out for singing or doing anything in public." But by God's grace I held on to my trust that I was rooted in God's love and could learn and grow. I kept trying. God's grace came to me through some of you—you lifted me up when I fell. You saw something in me when I couldn't. And now—years later—by God's grace I can be one of your kindly gardeners—and you mine. Together we trust God's abundance and claim God's blessing spoken through the prophet Jeremiah:

Blessed are those who trust in God, whose trust is God They shall be like a tree planted by water, sending out its roots by the stream. Jeremiah 17:7

Now we are on 23 and see the *Welcome to Michigan* sign—Oh Michigan, My Michigan. At the Michigan welcome center we switch drivers. And as soon as I remark that there have been no accidents, a tail-gating car in the passing lane causes an accident. I think: How quickly disaster strikes. How quickly we get cut down. Let all who think they stand take heed lest they fall. Wait—isn't that from the epistle for March 3?

If you think you are standing, watch out that you do not fall. No testing has overtaken you that is not common to everyone. God is trustworthy, and God will not let you be tested beyond your strength, but with the testing, God will also provide the way out so that you may be able to endure it. I Corinth. 11:12

Home at last after 16 hours on the road. We empty the car of the detritus of traveling. I find my sermon work folder unopened. I hold it for a moment realizing that by just bringing it and remembering the parable of the fig tree I planted a seed in my mind. While we were driving the seed took root and grew. I nurtured and tended the seedling sermon as the gardener cared for the fig tree. Now I need just write it. By God's grace I can trust it will blossom and bear fruit. Yet another lesson in God's grace.

God's grace sustains us all through the soul's winter—through all our trials. With roots growing down to God's grace we withstand the barren times. And—by god's grace—we bear fruit—each of us according to what God intends for us.

Give Thanks for the Gift of Life

Hostility

GIVE THANKS FOR THE GIFT OF LIFE

Troubled by the hostility I see in the world, I begin to reflect upon the prayer of Jesus in John 17: *Holy Father, protect in your name those whom you have given me, that they may be one, as we are one.* And I find myself remembering a Mother's Day with my family at Lake Michigan. We make our way through the woods to the top of the dunes at Meinert County Park. I feel the warmth of the sun on my back. I hear birdsong and voices. I feel the breeze on my skin. I see the brook meandering its way into the lake. Turning I see the woods and farmlands that separate the lakeshore from the nearest towns. And I find myself whispering, "My God, how great you are!" As my loved ones, one at a time, run down the dune to the lake, I sit alone dodging kicked up sand and remembering those who used to sit on the dune with us. I lift my tearful eyes skyward and see the clouds and the shadow of the moon. And the words of Psalm 8 come to mind:

O God, our Sovereign, how majestic is your name in all the earth! You have set your glory above the heavens. Out of the mouths of babes and infants you have made a bulwark to still the enemy and the avenger. . . . When I look at your heavens, the work of your fingers, the moon and the stars that you have established; what are human beings that you are mindful of them, mortals that you care for them? Yet you have made them a little lower than God, and crowned them with glory and honor. You have made them caretakers of the works of your hands.

. . . I am amazed that the Creator is mindful of us! Mindful of God's grace, we thank God for the gift of life.

As I continue to reflect upon the prayer of Jesus: *Holy Father, protect in your name those whom you have given me, that they may be one, as we are one,* I remember driving home to Clare. We are almost home when I tell my husband that I feel sad because we have seen no blue herons. As if on cue, he points and says, "Look!" And there it is— a great blue heron in flight. And I suddenly realize that not only is God mindful of us, but God has created us to be mindful people. Sights, sounds and smells trigger memories. Mindful of our joyful and sorrowful experiences, we thank God for the gift of life.

As I continue to reflect upon the prayer of Jesus: *Holy Father, protect in your name those whom you have given me, that they may be one, as we are one,* I remember sitting at my picnic table at the lake writing a sermon. Suddenly I am startled by a loud buzzing. I think, "What a huge bee!" But it isn't a bee. It is a hummingbird. And I am amazed by the variety of birds, plants and animals. Mindful of the works of God's hands, we thank God for the gift of life.

As I continue to reflect upon the prayer of Jesus: *Holy Father, protect in your name those whom you have given me, that they may be one, as we are one,* I remember watching hummingbirds at the feeder. There is definitely a pecking order! And it seems to me that human beings often do not rise much above this "instinct" for power and domination. We war amongst ourselves. I find myself asking, "Why is this so?" And the words of Romans 8 come to mind:

What, then, are we to say about these things? If God is for us, who is against us? . . . Who will separate us from the love of Christ? Will hardship, or distress, or persecution, or famine, or nakedness, or peril, or sword? . . . No, in all these things we are more that conquerors through Christ who loved us. For I am convinced that neither death, nor life, nor angels, nor rulers, nor things present, nor things to come, nor powers, nor height, nor depth, nor anything else in all creation will be able to separate us from the love of God in Christ Jesus our Lord.

Mindful of these ancient words of comfort, we thank God for the gift of life.

As I continue to reflect upon the prayer of Jesus: *Holy Father, protect in your name those whom you have given me, that they may be one, as we are one,* I marvel that God is mindful of us. I marvel that we—created in God's image—are mindful people. And I pray that we may be of one mind with God, respecting and honoring God's call to care for the universe. Mindful of the wonders of the universe, we thank God for the gift of life.

Hurry up and wait!

Impatience

HURRY UP AND WAIT

I've been waiting—not very patiently—for a replacement part for a chair. Four weeks became six. Six became eight. Eight became ten. Finally the part is here! But now I must wait for the technician to phone and arrange an installation date. Two days have become three. Three have become four. And I anticipate having to dial yet another 1-800 number to talk to some machine in order to find out I'll have to wait some more!

I ask myself, "why is it so hard to wait?" Perhaps it's because we feel so powerless. Powerlessness leads to helplessness. Helplessness leads to fear. Fear leads to anger. Soon we are immersed in a sea of roiling feelings that make us feel demoralized and hopeless. Maybe—not being able to influence the true culprit—we begin to release our pent up feelings on some hapless bystander (a spouse, for example) who has no idea what he or she has done wrong.

I chide myself for my impatience. After all I'm waiting for something that seems rather insignificant. But, significant or not, waiting is difficult on many levels: Emotional, psychological, physical and spiritual. Maybe all the little annoyances that require waiting remind us of all the waiting we have had to do for something that is truly significant and life-altering:

Waiting for a job interview.

Waiting for a call-back after a job interview.

Waiting for a test result or diagnosis.

Waiting through chemotherapy or radiation.

Waiting for a loved one to return home safely.

Waiting for someone to stop tormenting you.

Waiting for God to open a window when a door has closed.

Waiting seems to be part of the human condition. We all have to endure it. In my times of waiting I have found endurance and great comfort in trusting that I am a child of God and that God is waiting with me. I often recite Psalm 27—slowly and thoughtfully.

> *God is my light and my salvation; whom shall I fear?*
> *God is the stronghold of my life; of whom shall I be afraid?*
> *Though an army encamp against me, my heart shall not fear.*
> *Though war rise up against me, yet will I be confident.*
> *. . . For God will hide me in God's shelter in the day of trouble;*
> *God will conceal me under the cover of God's tent;*
> *God will set me high on a rock.*
> *Now my head is lifted up above my enemies all around me.*
> *. . . I believe that I shall see the goodness*
> *of God in the land of the living.*
> *Wait for God, be strong; let your heart take courage,*
> *Wait for God!*

Are you waiting for something—patiently or impatiently? Write the words, "Wait for God, be strong; let your heart take courage. Wait for God." Carry the words with you as an affirmation. Take a deep breath. <u>Let</u> your heart take courage. <u>Let</u> yourself feel your feelings. <u>Let</u> yourself go through the pain. <u>Let</u> yourself trust that you are not alone. <u>Let</u> yourself trust that God is with you.

Through It All

Life after Death

THROUGH IT ALL

In the Apostle's Creed we say that Jesus descended into hell and ascended into heaven. And it seems to me that those two extremes in Jesus' life mirror the extremes in our lives. We experience heavenly moments when everything seems to be wonderful and it is easy to believe in God and trust that God is good. And we experience hellish moments when we are in so much pain that we wonder whether—if there is a God—God has abandoned us. I'm not sure why life has to have such extremes, but this I know: Through it all—the heavens and the hells, beginnings and endings, living and dying, time and eternity—God is with us. How do I know? The Bible tells me so. The Psalmist sings in Psalm 139:

> *Oh God, you have searched me, and known me.*
> *You know when I sit down and when I rise up;*
> *You discern my thoughts from far away. . . .*
> *You hem me in, behind and before, and lay your hand upon me.*
> *Such knowledge is too wonderful for me; it*
> *is so high that I cannot attain it.*
> *Where can I go from your Spirit?*
> *Or where can I flee from your presence?*
> *If I ascend to heaven, you are there;*
> *if I make my bed in Sheol, you are there.*

If I take the wings of the morning and settle
at the farthest limits of the sea,
even there your hand shall lead me; and your
right hand shall hold me fast . . . .
For it was you who formed my inward parts;
You knit me together is my mother's womb.
I praise you, for I am fearfully and wonderfully made.
Wonderful are your works—that I know very well . . . .
Your eyes beheld my unformed substance.
In your book were written all the days that were
formed for me before they existed.
How weighty to me are your thoughts, O God!
How vast the sum of them!
I try to count them—they are more than the sand;
I come to the end—I am still with you. [Psalm 139]

I come to the end—I'm still with you. Through it all—the heavens and the hells, beginnings and endings, living and dying, time and eternity—God is with us.

I believe that we live at one and the same time in two worlds—the world of time and the world of timelessness—eternity. We already have one foot in eternity, but we often do not notice because we are caught up in the daily living of our lives. We think of our lives as time-lines that begin when we are born and end when we die. Occasionally the light breaks through and we experience a sense of "moreness" to life. As our bodies—made for temporary use—begin to fail, those moments of spiritual awareness seem to become more real. When we near death, the veil between time and eternity seems to be lifted and the soul makes its way home.

How the soul makes this transition we do not know. The writer to the Corinthian Christians uses nature to explain this mysterious transformation. The writer takes a grain of wheat and explains that we cannot see in the grain the plant that it will be. No—the seed is just a seed until it is planted. So it is with the human body. We cannot see in our temporary bodies the glory of what we will be in the resurrection. Then—in one of the most beautiful resurrection passages in the Bible the writer says:

Listen, I will tell you a mystery! We will not totally die, but we will
be totally changed, in a moment, in the twinkling of an eye, at the
last trumpet. For the trumpet will sound, and the dead will be raised
imperishable, and we will be changed. For this perishable body must
put on imperishability and this mortal body must put on immortality.
When this perishable body puts on imperishability, and this mortal
body puts on immortality, then the saying that is written will be fulfilled:
"Death has been swallowed up in victory."
Where, O death, is your victory? Where, O death, is your sting?"
. . . . thanks be to God, who gives the victory through
our Lord Jesus Christ. [I Corinthians 15]

Hymn writer Natalie Sleeth uses nature to describe this mystery in her "Hymn of Promise" written while her husband was dying of cancer and dedicated to him after his death:

*In the bulb there is a flower; in the seed, an apple tree;
In cocoons, a hidden promise: butterflies will soon be free!
In the cold and snow of winter there's a spring that waits to be,
Unrevealed until its season, something God alone can see.

There's a song in every silence, seeking word and melody;
There's a dawn in every darkness, bringing hope to you and me.
From the past will come the future; what it holds a mystery,
Unrevealed until its season, something God alone can see.

In our end is our beginning; in our time, infinity;
In our doubt there is believing; in our life, eternity.
In our death, a resurrection; at the last, a victory,
Unrevealed until its season, something yet unknown

Which God alone can see.

Through it all—the heavens and the hells, beginnings
and endings, living and dying, time and eternity—
God is with us.

God is with us now. In word. In prayer. In music. In memories of
our loved ones. In stories shared. In gifts of cards, food and flowers. In
the touch of a hand. In our tears and laughter. In the sight of a flower
pushing through the snow. In the feeling of the sunlight on our faces.
In all the seasons of life.

Through it all—the heavens and the hells, beginnings
and endings, living and dying, time and eternity—
God is with us.

AND—our loved ones who have died are with God. For them all
sickness and sorrow are ended and death itself is past and they have
entered the home where all God's people gather in peace. For this we
say, "Thanks be to God."

An Attitude of Gratitude

Losses

An Attitude of Gratitude

There's a story about a woman who has the opportunity to talk to God face to face. She asks God, "how much is a million dollars worth to you?" God answers, "A million dollars? Why, not more than a penny." The woman asks, "And what is a million years worth to you?" God answers, "A million years?—"why not more than a second." And the woman says, "Well—can I have a million dollars?" God responds, "Sure—in a second." Well, try as we might, we cannot fully comprehend eternal truths—especially when it comes to money and possessions.

What we <u>can</u> try to wrap our minds around is the concept that everything is a gift from God—a gift entrusted into our keeping. One of my favorite offertory prayers says it all: "We give to you what you have first given us—our selves, our time, our possessions—signs of your gracious love. Receive them for the sake of him who offered himself for us—Jesus Christ our Lord." When we can pray this prayer in a heartfelt manner we have some people call "an attitude of gratitude." This attitude is not a feeling but a state of mind.

Question is—how do we cultivate this attitude of gratitude? Think, for a moment about how you feel when you have enough money. Happy? Secure? Surprised? I usually start worrying that I forgot to pay a bill! In good times it is fairly easy to have an attitude of gratitude because we <u>feel</u> grateful. Now, how do you feel when money is low? Unhappy? Insecure? Anxious? In hard times it's more difficult to have an attitude of gratitude because we don't <u>feel</u> grateful.

Yet most of us—when in need—can GET help from a friend, a relative, government, the church. But how would you feel if there was no one to help and even the church turned its back on you? That's how it was for widows at the time of Mark's gospel. At that time the Scribes had risen to a place of great power. They were experts in Jewish Law. Some of them, apparently, had become scam artists. Reading death notices, they made note of the names of widows— who, by law, inherited at least their houses. Then they claimed the widow's house as *corban* or set aside for God. That's why—according to Mark's gospel—Jesus says the scribes "devoured widows' houses." He taught,

"Beware of the Scribes, who like to walk around in long robes, and to be greeted with respect in the marketplaces, and to have the best seats in the synagogues and places of honor at banquets! They devour widows' houses and for the sake of appearance say long prayers. They will receive the greater condemnation."

Then he sat down opposite the treasury and watched the crowd putting money into the treasury. Many rich people put in large sums. A poor widow came and put in two small copper coins, which are worth a penny. Then he called his disciples and said to them, "Truly I tell you, this poor widow has put in more than all those who are contributing to the treasury. For all of them have contributed out of their abundance; but she out of her poverty has put in everything she had, all she had to live on."(Mark 12:43-44)

And why would that poor widow have an attitude of gratitude? Why would she share?

—Perhaps she treasured Jesus' teaching in the Sermon on the Mt.

Do not store up for yourselves treasures on earth, where moth and rust consume and where thieves break in and steal; but store up for your selves treasures in heaven where neither moth nor rust consumes and

where thieves do not break in and steal. For where your treasure is, there your heart will be also. Matthew 6:19

—Perhaps she treasured the story of the widow of Zarephath whose jar of meal and jug of oil never failed because she was willing to share what she had with the prophet Elijah in his hour of need.

—Perhaps she focused on the positive. Reminds me the lyrics of the old gospel song my mom used to sing:

When upon life's billows you are tempest tossed, when you are discouraged, thinking all is lost, Count your many blessings—name them one by one, and it will surprise you what the Lord hath done . . . . Johnson Oatman Jr.

And how about us? Do we treasure Jesus' words and the story of the widow of Zarephath? Do we focus on the positive? Do we count our blessings? Do we have an attitude of gratitude? There are certainly times in our lives when we are "tempest tossed and we are discouraged thinking all is lost." Today we need only recall the images Hurricane Sandy to be reminded of people whose lives have been literally tempest tossed. Yet I am struck by the news interview with a New Jersey man saying—through his tears, "We've lost everything, but we are alive." That's an attitude of gratitude! Which is not to say, he doesn't feel overwhelmed, doesn't feel angry, doesn't feel sad, doesn't feel guilty, doesn't feel depressed. Yet he seems to understand at a very deep level that life is a gift.

And it is! Life is a gift! Do you accept the gift? That's the question I ask myself EVERY day. I wake up often during the night having to stretch arthritic joints. But at first light I imagine God saying to me "You've been given another day—do you accept the gift?" I answer, "Yes—I accept the gift." Then I slowly lever myself onto my aching joints. And no matter what the day brings, I am strengthened by my mindset—my attitude of gratitude.

Sometimes we get infected by a virus called "scarcity thinking"—a fear-based disease. This mindset weakens us. We get all penny-pinching and miserly. But we are called to be a love-based people—strengthened by the knowledge that we are richly blessed by God. God calls us "children of God!" We inherit God's promises!

Rich in so many ways and caretakers of all God has entrusted to us, we pray from a mindset—an attitude of gratitude: God, we give to you what you have first given us—ourselves, our time, our possessions—signs of your gracious love. Receive them for the sake of him who offered himself for us.

Showers of Blessing

Messiness

SHOWERS OF BLESSING

It is Valentine's Day and my husband and I begin driving from Clare to Boston. Chased through Michigan and Ohio by threatening storms we take the scenic route through Pennsylvania to the Washington D.C. area to spend time with our granddaughter who is a student at George Mason University. With her we stroll the streets of the Capital in blue jeans and sweaters.

Thankful for unseasonably good weather we work up the courage to drive from D.C. to Boston through the megapolis that lies between. As the song goes, the "traffic is terrific," but we make it with the help of a GPS and our time-worn strategy of switching drivers every two hours.

I feel my adrenalin level rise as we approach Boston with its spider web of streets and impatient drivers. It seems as if our Michigan license plate is an invitation to tailgaters! Turning onto our daughter's street—reduced to one lane by six foot high piles of snow and ice—we find ourselves playing "chicken" with a pickup truck. I win only because we can turn into the parking lot before the truck reaches us.

Negotiating the streets of Boston becomes easier because our daughter does the driving—by mutual consent and much to my relief. A two-week thaw has done very little to reduce the piles of snow and interesting things have begun to appear. It look like some kind of bizarre garden sprouting discarded Christmas trees, garbage bags, lost gloves and shopping carts along the streets of the city.

As the thaw ends and we huddle against the wind and cold and snow, everything looks pristine and clean again and I begin to wonder if something similar happens in our lives. Crises pile up. Functioning on excess adrenalin, we plow the detritus aside so we can create a way through the mess. As stresses ease, the troubling issues we hoped we had left behind reappear—all the dirtier for having been buried.

Then—by God's grace—the showers of blessing come cleansing and purifying. We can cope once again with the duality in our lives. The ugly and the beautiful. The dirty and the clean. The joyful and the sorrowful. We remember God's promise in Ezekiel 43:26: "I will send down showers in their season; they shall be showers of blessing." And we sing with Daniel W. Whittle and James McGranahan:

> "*There shall be showers of blessing*"—*this is the promise of love;*
> *There shall be seasons refreshing, sent from the Savior above.*
> *Showers of blessing, showers of blessing we need;*
> *Mercy-drops round us are falling, but for the showers we plead.*

Today tell God about your life—all of it. Cover nothing up. Let God's mercy cleanse your soul.

As a Mother Comforts Her Child

Mother's Day

AS A MOTHER COMFORTS HER CHILD

So I will comfort you;
*You shall be comforted . . . .*Isaiah 66:13

There was a young mother with two daughters. The older daughter had recently had surgery at a hospital in Iowa. The young mother had stayed with the toddler holding her after surgery, walking the floors with her, becoming exhausted from the strain. But she hadn't cared about the fatigue or the bloodstains on her clothing. She heard her child's cry and responded to her in her hour of need. And the child was comforted.

When the family moved to Long Island, the young mother learned that the younger daughter, now one year old, needed surgery on both eyes and the mother planned to stay with her child during the ordeal. But things were different in this hospital. Parents were told, "Children do better without their parents. They cry less." Parents were expected to leave their children at the hospital and pick them up in two days. The young mother who had worked for a Dr. as a nurse-receptionist for five years appealed to the hospital authorities hoping they would bend the rules and allow her to stay. When that appeal failed, she looked for support from family and friends. They all sympathized and said, "There's nothing more you can do." Some said, "Maybe the hospital is right. Maybe you should just obey the rules." At night she found no relief from her anguish. As she tossed and turned she cried. As she cried she prayed. As she prayed she recalled the philosophy of the Martin Luther King: "When the laws of the land do not protect the rights of the people they are meant to serve, one must call upon a higher law—God's love."

The next morning she went to the toy box where the children kept their dress-up clothes and dug out an old white uniform, white shoes and white hose. In her jewelry box she found her student nurse pin. She washed and ironed her clothes and polished her shoes and on the day of her baby's admission to the hospital the young mother dressed carefully in her nurse's clothing and stayed at the hospital with her child. It was a very difficult time for the young mother. It was the first time she actively defied authority. But she believed the hospital was wrong and that her baby needed her.

When the child came from surgery, both eyes were patched. Beside her lay her stuffed snoopy dog whose eyes were also patched. Both of the baby's arms were splinted to prevent her from tearing the bandages from her eyes. She lay there arms outstretched and helpless like a little Christ figure. And the young mother, hearing her child whimper and seeing the little body helplessly tied gently undid the splints promising the Dr. that she would hold the child and prevent her from tearing at the bandages. And the child, unable to see, heard her mother's voice, "Sh-sh! It's OK! Mommy's here. Sh-sh!" And the young mother held her child and walked the floors and endured the glares of some of the staff because she heard her child's cry and responded to her in her hour of need. And the child was comforted.

The young mother—now an old woman—looks back upon the times in her life when her own eyes were covered with despair and her arms helplessly tied by fear and she can see that God has <u>always</u> heard her cries and responded to her in her hour of need. And she is comforted. She rejoices with the Psalmist:

I love God, because God has heard my voice
and has heard my supplications.
Because God inclined an ear to me,
Therefore I will call on God as long as I live. Psalm 116

Filter Out the Negative

Negativity

FILTER OUT THE NEGATIVE

I am sitting in the waiting room reading while my car is being serviced and suddenly the mechanic comes into the room holding the filter from my car. He says, "Let me hold this filter up to the light so you can see how dirty it is." Before I can say, "No thank you," he lifts it. I shrink back as bugs and dirt float to the floor. He tells me the hepa filter behind the motor filter is very dirty too and if I have an allergy to ragweed—which I do—my filter system is not doing me much good. I recall how much I sneezed after a two hour car trip a few days ago. It all makes sense now. Of course, I decide I need to replace both filters no matter the cost.

Driving home from the dealership I begin to think about the "filters" we have in our lives. Denial comes to mind. Maybe we hear scary news from a Doctor and—in self-protection mode—decide it's not so bad. Maybe we fear for a relationship and—to protect or defend ourselves or a loved one—deny the truth. Denial is a powerful filter that—in its most positive sense—protects us until we are mentally ready to face reality.

There seems to be so much negativity in life. I turn on the television and am immediately confronted by what seems a preoccupation with revenge, betrayal and gossip in programming and in talk shows. Who among us hasn't been in the presence of joy killers—people who seem to suck the positive out of life?

So—how do we filter out the negative and let in the positive? We reflect upon our past experiences and re-vision our life story. When I reflect upon my life, I remember with shame how I have damaged people by what I have done or said and how I have been damaged by what people have said or done. But when I look back, I realize that it is often the people I consider my enemies who have taught me the most. While I neither condone nor appreciate hurtful words or actions I can appreciate what I have learned from them.

How do we filter out the negative and let in the positive? We practice affirmations like the one that occurred to me recently: *Be less interested in what bugs you about people than in what you appreciate about them.* I repeat this affirmation every day—especially during the times when I am stressed and fatigued and it is so easy to dwell on the negative.

How do we filter out the negative and let in the positive? We take it easy on ourselves—allowing ourselves to have our feelings. It is natural to feel angry when sucker-punched. HAVE the feeling and then let it pass before saying something regrettable.

How do we filter out the negative and let in the positive? We focus on the positive. That is the lesson from Philippians 4:8:

Whatever is true, whatever is honorable, whatever is pure, whatever is just, whatever is pure, whatever is pleasing, whatever is commendable, if there is any excellence and if there is anything worthy of praise, think about these things.

Negativity can make us soul sick. We need to replace the filters of our souls. Choose to be less interested in what bugs you about people than in what you appreciate about them. Having made the choice,

Act kindly—
Speak Kindly—
Think kindly.

Strangers in a Strange Land

New Beginnings

STRANGERS IN A STRANGE LAND

While doing some New Year cleaning I come upon a scrapbook I made after returning home from an entirely unexpected trip to Germany and the Netherlands. Suddenly I find myself transported back in time.

It's August, 2001 and my husband and I are completely lost in the Netherlands. Though it is our ancestral home we feel as if we are strangers in a strange land. We've been driving around for hours in our rental car trying to reach Amsterdam in time to board our flight home. Now we've made a wrong turn onto a beautifully paved, narrow road and we suddenly realize we are on a bicycle road parallel to the highway—who knew some countries actually protect cyclists by creating roads just for them! We quickly realize our mistake and pull into a parking lot to get our bearings. Finally on the correct road we resume our wanderings.

By now I feel utterly bewildered and I convince my husband to stop at a gas station for snacks, coffee and directions. In the store my six-word Dutch vocabulary is of no use whatsoever! But my husband finds someone who explains the directions in English while I wait in line to pay for snacks and coffee. I've given up trying to figure out just how the Dutch coins translate into dollars and—feeling completely inadequate—simply give the cashier all the coins in my hand hoping she will take what she needs and give me the correct change.

Finally—snacks in hand—I fumble my way out of the store grateful that my husband has pulled up to the door and is waiting for me. I get into the passenger seat, close the car door, reach for my seatbelt, latch it and say, "I'm so relieved!" To my surprise my husband responds to me in Dutch! I look at him—it's not my husband! It suddenly dawns on me that I am in some Dutch guy's car. I say profoundly, "Oh! You're not my husband!"

The guy responds in Dutch and I apologize in English. Embarrassed as can be I get out of the car—again juggling my goodies and slopping the coffee—and spy my husband waving to me from across the parking lot. He pulls up and I get in the right car which looks a lot like the Dutch guy's car. All I can say is, "I hope you got directions 'cause I just want to go home!"

Now—twelve years later—I put away my scrapbook laughing at the memory. What was so frightening at the time now seems hilarious. The passage of time has allowed me to put things in perspective. But I'll always remember just how lost, bewildered, and inadequate I felt. I realize that—at the time—my husband and I had jobs at home—a secure income. We were not penniless. Now I find myself feeling compassion towards people who must move to places whose language they do not speak. Whose customs they do not know. Where there is no secure job waiting for them and no home to which they can return. How utterly lost, bewildered and inadequate they must feel—strangers in a strange land.

Of course, we can all tap into this feeling. Every change—positive or negative—requires adjustment. Chaim Potok wrote in one of his novels, "All beginnings are difficult."

We begin picking up the pieces after a divorce or after the death of a loved one and we feel lost, bewildered and inadequate—strangers in a strange land.

We begin a time of searching for or training for a new job and feel lost, bewildered and inadequate—strangers in a strange land.

We begin life as a college student or start a new school term and we feel lost, bewildered and inadequate—strangers in a strange land.

We begin to welcome a newborn into the family and we feel lost, bewildered and inadequate—strangers in a strange land.

We begin a recovery program and we feel lost, bewildered and inadequate—strangers in a strange land.

We begin living with a chronic illness and feel lost, bewildered and inadequate—strangers in a strange land.

So many beginnings! So many adjustments! But now—from my perspective as an older woman—I look back and see that all of my beginnings—joyful and sorrowful—are sacred. I see God's guiding hand—even in those times when I have felt the most lost, bewildered and inadequate—a stranger in a strange land.

Truly all things work together for good to those who love God. Romans 8

Be at Peace

Regret

BE AT PEACE

Index cards lie on my bedside stand along with my book and alarm clock. Index cards with words calling me away from a lifetime of middle-of-the night regret and worry: "Why did I say that?!" "How could I have done that?!" Index cards with comforting words calling me to be at peace because God is with me. Words from Joshua 1: *Be strong and courageous; do not be frightened or dismayed, for the Lord your God is with you wherever you go.* Words from Philippians 4: *God is near, do not worry about anything, but in everything by prayer and supplication with thanksgiving let your requests be made known to God. And the peace of God, which surpasses all understanding, will guard your hearts and your minds in Christ Jesus.*

Our Bible lies on the table. Our Bible opened to Isaiah 11. Prophetic words calling us away from fear and anxiety about nuclear holocaust, war, blizzards and floods. Prophetic words calling us to be at peace because the world is in God's hands and God's intention is to bring about a peaceable kingdom because *a shoot shall come from the stump of Jesse . . . . The spirit of the Lord shall rest upon him. . . . He shall . . . decide with equity for the gentle of the earth. The wolf shall live with the lamb, the leopard shall lie down with the kid, the calf and the lion and the fatling together, and a little child shall lead them. The cow and the bear shall graze, their young shall lie down together; and the lion shall eat straw like the ox. The nursing child shall play over the home of the asp . . .*

. They will not hurt or destroy on all my holy mountain; for the earth will be full of the knowledge of the Lord as the waters cover the sea.

Advent and Christmas songs and carols fill the air in every shopping center, gas station and restaurant . Carols—musical words—calling us away from the stress and busyness of the season. The worry about buying just the right gift or getting just what we want. Musical words calling us to be at peace because God has already given us the best gift—Immanuel, God with us. The Word made flesh.

Hail, Hail, the Word made flesh—the babe, the son of Mary . . . .
Ring silver bells, merrily ring—tell all the world Jesus is King . . . .
Lo, how a rose e'er blooming from tender stem hath sprung!
Of Jesse's lineage coming as saints of old have sung . . . .

Crosses hang on the walls of our churches and homes. We wear them as jewelry. Crosses—symbolic words—calling us away from doubt and despair. Symbolic words calling us to be at peace because we trust that *by dying Christ defeated death and by rising he opened to us the gates of everlasting life.* For he said, according to John 14,

Do not let your hearts be troubled. Trust God, trust also in me.
In my Father's house there are many dwelling places.
If it were not so would I have told you that
I go to prepare a place for you?
And if I go and prepare a place for you,
I will come again and will take you to myself, so
that where I am, there you may be also . . . .
I have said these things to you while I am still with you.
But the Helper, the Holy Spirit, whom the Father will send in my name,
will teach you everything, and remind you of all that I have said to you.
Peace I leave with you; my peace I give to you.
I do not give to you as the world gives.
Do not let your hearts be troubled, and do not let them be afraid.

God's voice is sounding all around us. Do you hear? God is calling us away from regret and worry, fear and anxiety, stress and busyness, doubt and despair. God is calling us to be at peace.

> *Now may the God of hope fill you with all joy and*
> *peace in believing that you may abound in hope by*
> *the power of the Holy Spirit.* Romans 15:13

This Little Light of Mine

Self-doubt

THIS LITTLE LIGHT OF MINE

As a person who prefers a slower pace and time for quiet reflection I sometimes feel like I don't quite belong. Everyone seems to move faster than I. Last weekend, for example, I drive to our trailer on the shores of Lake Michigan and when I arrive, every trailer is deserted and I know everyone is at the beach. In the distance I hear waves crashing and I rightfully assume my husband, children and grandchildren are jumping them. I think about strolling to the beach but the idea of watching my loved ones tossed by the waves and defying rip currents does not appeal to me. Instead I take advantage of the unusual quiet and sit with my crossword puzzle and book. Within minutes my husband returns looking exhilarated from his battle with Lake Michigan, and I learn that this is their second time in the water. Or, maybe, it was one big time in the water with a short break for lunch.

One by one my family returns from the beach and we chat while everyone rests. But before I know it chat time—which I love—is over and everyone is moving on to the next activity. I eat my supper taking—of course—longer than anyone else. I feel a bit bewildered and fatigued by the high energy level around me.

That night when he and I are alone I remark to my husband, "It's as if my family is the world and I am the moon. I'm there on the fringes. Now you see me. Now you don't. It makes me feel a bit sad." But my spirits rise as I consider the significance of the moon in our universe. It is actually frightening to think of what would happen to the world without the moon. A fact charmingly illustrated in the animated movie *Despicable Me* in which someone attempts to shrink and steal the moon. And, of course, nothing is right until the moon is replaced.

So, in terms of my place in my family, and my community I feel comforted by the lesson from nature. I am an important part of the system even when I am just sitting quietly. Even when I am barely noticed. Even when I am alone meditating and praying. After all, even the quiet, reflective person shines brightly all of the time even though the glow might appear to be periodic to the observer.

It takes all kinds of things to keep the universe balanced. It takes all kinds of people to care for the universe. And it's all in God's hands.

> *The whole world is in God's hands.*
> *You and I, brother, are in God's hands.*
> *You and I, sister, are in God's hands.*
> *The moon and the stars are in God's hands.*
> *The itty-bitty baby is in God's hands.*
> *The whole world's in God's hands.*

Next time you are feeling like you don't belong, remember that you are unique and beautiful. Your uniqueness and beauty make the universe a better place. Don't be afraid to let your light shine—even if it seems less bright than that of the people around you.

God Walks with Us

Stress

GOD WALKS WITH US

As I read the story of Nathaniel's call to follow Christ, I am struck by the fact that Jesus is aware of Nate before Nate is aware of Jesus. This is an awesome, transformative revelation for Nate. And it is much the same for me. At a spiritual level I realize I am eternally known by God. For me, then, the call to follow Christ is a call to <u>let</u> my life be transformed by the knowledge that God walks with me.

As I pass through life's transitions I can look back and see God's presence. And I can allow myself to project into the future the confidence that God will continue to be present to me. The call to follow Christ remains a call to let my life be transformed—in every way—by the knowledge that God walks with me.

As I live with the vulnerability of day-to-day life I remember God walks with me and I pray with the anonymous poet:

I am weak, but Thou art strong;
Jesus, keep me from all wrong;
I'll be satisfied as long
As I walk, let me walk close to Thee.

As I live with the stress of day-to-day life I remember God walks with me and I pray:

Through this world of toil and snares,
If I falter, Lord, who cares?
Who with me my burden shares?
None but Thee, dear Lord, none but Thee.

As I live with the knowledge of my mortality I
remember God walks with me and I pray:

When my feeble life is o'er,
Time for me will be no more;
Guide me gently, safely o'er
To Thy kingdom's shore, to Thy shore.

Do you hear God calling you? Don't worry so much about
whether you are following correctly or doing everything you should!
Instead, remember God knows you eternally and is already walking
with you. Let this knowledge be a light upon your path.

The call to follow Christ is a call to let your life be transformed
by the knowledge that God walks with you. Rest in the awareness of
God's presence and pray with the hymnist:

Just a closer walk with Thee,
Grant, it, Jesus is my plea,
Daily walking close to Thee,
Let it be, dear Lord, let it be.

(public domain poem based
upon II Corinthians 13:4)

You are My Child—the Beloved

Transition

You Are My Child—the Beloved

As I prepared for today I opened my Bible and started at the beginning—an Old Testament lesson from Genesis—God's rainbow promise. To place it historically—Jesus was born roughly 2000 years ago and his ancestors Abraham and Sarah 4000 years ago. Genesis eventually tells their story but begins with stories that cannot be dated: Creation, the fall of humankind into sin, the flood—God washing sin from the world beginning again. As the story goes, Noah—trusting God—builds a huge boat—the Ark—and gathers a male and a female of every kind of animal into the Ark before the rain begins to fall. And (according to oral tradition) Noah's wife Naamah gathers seeds and plant life.

As I reflected upon Noah's and Naamah's trust in God I found myself singing:

If you but trust in God to Guide you with
hopeful heart through all your days.
You will find strength—with God beside you—
to bear the worst of evil days.
For those who trust God's changeless love
Build on a rock that will not move.

And I remembered a time when I boarded a vessel—not an

Ark—but a plane. In NYC. It was raining pitchforks and I was terrified about the flight. I began to pray I would reach my destination. I breathed deeply and entrusted my life to God. The plane safely left the ground and soared through the clouds and, suddenly, the sun was blinding me. I looked down and saw no buildings, no people, no land—just the tops of the clouds—

And I thought, "It must have been something like this for Noah and Naamah and their kids. They lived through the terror of 40 days and nights of rain—by the way, in the Bible, the number 40 is Bible talk for "a long time"—a long time that culminates when the time is right. For 150 days the ark floats and in moments of sunshine Noah and Naamah look down and see no buildings, no people, no land—just water. Then—bump—Mt. Ararat and 40 days and nights of receding water revealing the destruction left by the flood. At last Noah, *et al*, leave the Ark and the process of renewal begins with an astonishing promise from God. "I am establishing my covenant with you and your descendants after you AND with every living creature that is with you that never again shall all living creatures be cut off by the waters of a flood and never again shall there be a flood to destroy the earth. . . . I have set my bow in the clouds, and it shall be a sign of the covenant between me and the earth . . . . When the bow is in the clouds, I will see it and remember the everlasting covenant between me and every living creature of all flesh that is on the earth."

I closed my eyes and prayed for us—that we would remember God's rainbow promise and choose to trust God is guiding us.

I opened my Bible and read the gospel lesson. Mark—regarded by scholars as the earliest gospel. Filled with the word "immediately" Mark quickly reminds his listeners of Jesus' authority: Jesus is baptized and called by God. Jesus is initiated and trained with the required wilderness experience—40 days and nights, by the way. And, with his cousin JB imprisoned, Jesus takes up the mantle of Messiah—the promised one—and proclaims the good news telling people "the time is fulfilled, and the Kingdom of God has come near, repent, and trust in the good news."

I can just see Jesus in the river Jordan—rising from the water. I can see the clouds parted and the Spirit descending in the form of a dove. I can hear the voice from heaven, "You are my son, the beloved, with you I am well pleased." I can see Jesus immediately retreating to the desert—feel the sun and sand. Experience his fear of wild animals. Tremble at the power of Satan tempting him. And sense his relief as the angels minister to him. I can hear the authority in his voice as he begins his ministry.

I closed my eyes and prayed for us—that we would remember God's rainbow promise, give thanks to Jesus for coming in fulfillment of promise and choose to trust God is guiding us.

I opened my bible and read the epistle—I Peter—and noticed he is asking us to remember that, just as the flood symbolized the washing away of sin from the earth, so does our baptism symbolize the washing away of our sin—in Christ. And I found myself singing:

I was there to hear your newborn cry—I'll be there when you are old—
I rejoiced the day you were baptized—to see your life unfold.

I closed my eyes and prayed for us—that we would remember God's rainbow promise, give thanks to Jesus for coming in fulfillment of promise, cherish our baptism and choose to trust God is guiding us.

I reflected, then, upon our lives—times when we are lost in the wilderness of our minds because something is ending and we can't see what is beginning. We're sick or someone we love is dreadfully sick. We're grieving the loss of a loved one through death or divorce. We've lost a job. We are being bullied or abused.

It seems to me that life is a weaving together of wilderness and Promised Land experiences. Even in the middle of a new wilderness experience we can look back and see the angels were ministering to us is in our other wilderness experiences and we can project into the future the confidence that God is guiding us in one way or another.

And I prayed for us that we would remember God's rainbow

promise, give thanks to Jesus for coming in fulfillment of promise, cherish our baptism and choose to trust God is guiding us.

Affirm your baptism every day this week. When you wash your hands, bathe or shower remember that God gives you what we need to live. God washes away your sins. You are born not just to your moms and dads but to God. "See what great love God has for us that we should be called children of God." And you are a child of God—God loves you. No one can take that away from you.

To this I say, "Thanks be to God."

Peace like a River in My Soul

Troubled Waters

PEACE LIKE A RIVER IN MY SOUL

I am trying to stay on my raft in icy cold Lake Michigan. The waves are wildly unpredictable! I worry about the children playing closer to shore and hope someone is watching them. There can be rip currents in weather like this. Now I notice my husband is lying on his raft oblivious to a huge wave coming towards him.

"Watch out!" I shout. He sits up, the wave hits and over he goes! He catches up to his raft which is somersaulting north.

Now he glares at me and yells, "I would have been just fine if you hadn't said anything!"

I realize he is right and turn my attention to staying on my own raft. I try to relax and go with the flow. Of course the sound of the waves keeps me from surrendering completely and I get dumped—again and again.

Onshore I grab my towel and—oops! There goes my raft somersaulting up the beach! I don't feel too embarrassed chasing it because everyone else is fighting the wind. It's all part of the beach entertainment package! Now I've had enough of the beach and walk up the road to the safety of my trailer. In the relative calm I begin to reflect upon advice from a book I read years ago: *Hope and Help for Your Nerves* by Claire Weekes. The author suggests not fighting so hard to resist feelings but rather accepting what you are feeling, floating through the feelings and letting time pass. Accept—float—let time pass. I pause to give thanks for the many times that a book or a thought or a person has entered my life at just the right time.

Back at the trailer I shower away the sand that seems to have found every nook and cranny in my body and take a moment to reflect upon the fact that at the time I found Claire Weeke's book I had been trying to deal with panic attacks. The harder I fought to maintain an inner calm the more anxious and exhausted I became. The book gave me the key. Not that it is easy to change a lifelong habit even when you have the key. Making a change takes years—even a lifetime of practice. Years of trying to stay on the raft. The words—accept, float and let time pass—have been a mantra for decades. This mantra helps me step back from the waves of feelings that overwhelm me. I think of it as a form of letting go and letting God.

In those moments of surrender I sense beneath the turbulence of my life what I would call a soul river—the deep, wide river of the water of life flowing from the throne of God. And I find myself singing my mom's favorite hymn:

When peace like a river attendeth my way, when sorrows like sea billows roll, whatever my lot Thou hast taught me to say, "It is well, it is well with my soul."

Researching the lyrics I learn that the poet, Horatio G. Spafford, wrote these soul-stirring words while mourning the loss of all four of his daughters in the sinking of the SS Ville du Havre.

We are all creatures of two worlds—the physical and the spiritual. As human beings we are subject to the storms of life—not just in terms of weather but also in terms of human experience. Sometimes we get knocked right off our rafts. It is so difficult! How comforting it is to trust that as spiritual beings we have underneath the turbulence of our lives the soul river—the deep wide river of God's love.

Sitting at my table thinking of the soul river I find myself recalling a lesson in my Greek class at seminary. The soul river (*patmos* in Greek) is the river of the vision in Revelation 22. This river flows from the throne of God and is never turbulent or polluted. It never floods. It never destroys. It never dries up. It is crystal clear. Pure and life-giving, it always nurtures and feeds. This is also the river envisioned in Ezekiel 47 where the prophet sees water flowing from below the threshold at the entrance of the temple: *On the banks on both sides of the river, there will grow all kinds of trees for food. Their leaves will not wither nor their fruit fall, but they will bear fresh fruit every month, because the water for them flows from the sanctuary. Their fruit will be for food, and their leaves for healing.*

I sit now safe in my comfy chair listening to the sound of the wind and waves and wondering about the lives of those who read these words. I don't know whether you are experiencing calm or turbulence at the moment. Most of us seem to balance both extremes at once. But this I know: You and I are children of God. Underneath our lives flows the soul river—the river of the water of life—the deep wide river of God's love.

If you are feeling knocked about by life, surrender to God.

Accept—float—Let time pass.

And you can sing with the hymnist, *I've Got peace like a river in my soul.*

Near to the Heart of God

Valentine's Day

NEAR TO THE HEART OF GOD

As I gaze through my kitchen window on yet ANOTHER snowy day the sun breaks through the clouds and touches a tiny blue glass heart I keep on the window sill and I find myself thinking "Valentine's Day is coming and I've barely recovered from Christmas!"

Like many other people who are shy by nature, I find it difficult— during any holiday—to maintain balance between noise and quiet. Don't get me wrong. I enjoy some hoopla as long as I have time to recover in silence.

And—like many other people who have lived as long as I—I find it emotionally exhausting to experience all the joyful and painful memories prompted by holidays.

Sometimes it seems to me that Valentine's Day is

Just another day for those who have lost loved ones to feel bereft.
Just another day for those who have lost work to feel anxious.
Just another day for those who have lost health to feel afraid.
Just another day for those who have been abused to feel betrayed.
Just another day for those who have no
significant other to feel left out.

And ONE loss is usually not just ONE loss. I met a friend recently as I walked through the cemetery. Her husband died two years ago. I asked how she was doing and she said, "I miss him so much. It seems like I've not just lost him. I've lost the friends we shared. Everything is different."

As I continue to reflect upon loss my precious glass heart catches the sun's rays and I feel hopeful because the heart is a gift given to me so that I may remember that I am not alone. I hold the precious glass in my hand and say a prayer for the women and children it represents. And not just for the women and children it represents, but for all people who are suffering heartache. I hold the glass heart close to my heart and sing the old hymn by Cleland B. McAffee:

> *There is a place of quiet rest—near to the heart of God.*
> *A place where sin cannot molest—near to the heart of God.*
> *Oh Jesus, blest Redeemer, sent from the heart of God.*
> *Hold us who wait before thee—near to the heart of God.*

Valentines's Day is another day for you to be kind to yourself. Let yourself remember and feel your losses. Tell God how you feel.

Valentine's Day is another day for you to be kind to someone else. Reach out to another soul in need. Say a prayer. Send a card. Speak a kind word. In doing so we draw each other nearer to the heart of God.

Valentine's Day is another day to remember God's kindness to you. You are not alone! You ARE loved! You always HAVE been loved! You always WILL be loved.

Afterword: The Story of the Blue Heron

I don't remember ever feeling more loved and more frightened—at the same time—than the day I saw it—the great blue heron—standing in a drainage ditch alongside the country road.

It was a beautiful September day in 2000 and I was driving home from Lake Michigan to face a stressful Church schedule. My daughter had just phoned to say that tests confirmed that her cancer was back. My heart ached with the awareness of the journey ahead.

Sheri had first noticed shortness of breath while singing. Then came circulatory problems in her legs. Yet she went on stage at the Congregational Church to sing with her three friends who—together—formed the award winning Sweet Adeline's quartet called "Midas Touch." She had to use a crutch, but she stood and sang lead for the entire concert. I remember feeling proud of her courage! And when they sang "Amazing Grace," my soul began to pray. I asked God for a sign—"let me see a blue heron in flight."

Then—two days after the concert—came the drive home from Lake Michigan. On Indian Bay Rd. I saw it—the great blue heron. I felt loved because I had my sign—and frightened that the great bird was grounded. What did that mean?

Over the course of the next six months I pondered the meaning of the sign as we cared for our daughter. And I began to trust that God knew Sheri's higher good and that—whether she lived or died—her life was in God's hands.

During this time my husband and I kept up our pastoral work as best we could—so I found myself visiting a parishioner in the ICU of the same hospital we were frequenting with our daughter. The woman I visited couldn't read. A fact that became clear to me when she said she liked the Bible book—"Plasms". I was stymied. With all my extensive Bible knowledge I had never heard of "Plasms"—not even in the apochryphal books.

So I asked, " Can you tell about your favorite?"

"Oh," she said, "I like the one about the shepherd."

I realized that she meant Psalms and we recited Psalm 23 together. She talked about her son who had been hit by a car and killed several years before. Then—she told me she knew my daughter was still alive but she had seen her in heaven.

Taken aback, I said, "Tell me your dream."

"Well," she said, "In the dream I saw your daughter with my son in heaven. Your daughter asked me to tell you she is OK. It is so beautiful in heaven."

Touched by her willingness to share this precious dream with me, I asked her if she was looking forward to seeing her son.

"Oh yes!" she said. "I can't wait."

I asked her how she helped herself when she felt overwhelmed about her own failing health.

"Well," she said, "I sing my favorite song: *I'll fly away*. Do you know it?"

"Not well." I said, "can you sing a little for me?'

And she began to sing about flying away when her life is over. Flying away to "life's celestial shore."

Sheri, too, had dreams of flying away. She said she was in a tent on the shore of Lake Michigan. In the tent were many beautiful birds. And then it got scary because the birds wanted to get out of the tent and they couldn't find a way.

I said, "Sounds like your soul is getting tired of the sickness your body is suffering."

Then, on April 11, 2001—a cold, drizzly, foggy day—her body

gave way. I've never felt such anguish. It was as if the weather invaded my body and soul.

My husband and I followed the hearse from the hospital to Clare and I prayed, "Let me know all is well with Sheri's soul."

Amazingly—a blue heron flew over the hearse directly in front of us. I felt my spirits rise. Her soul was free.

Many people heard that story in the following days. I began to receive drawings and carvings of blue herons. It seemed we saw them everywhere! Of course, in Michigan, herons are a seasonal bird arriving when snow stops and leaving before it resumes. April 11 was very early for heron sightings.

Now—twelve years later—I see far fewer herons. Perhaps I am just not looking so intently. Perhaps I have outgrown the need for such encouragement. Still—whenever the sad memories come—I think,"Haven't seen a blue heron in a while." And there one is—in flight.

I believe God reaches out to us in mysterious ways. My prayer is this: May you be open to the little and big ways God is touching you and leading you.

Rev. Margaret Vredeveld

About the Author

Rev. Margaret Vredeveld is an ordained United Church of Christ pastor who served her congregation in Clare, Michigan for fourteen years.

Before serving as a pastor she worked as a musician and is a member of the National Association of Teachers of Singing, Inc.

Before working as a musician she worked as a nurse/office-manager for a General Practice Dr. in Grand Rapids, MI.

In retirement she continues to fulfill the office of pastor by presiding at funerals and weddings and by preaching occasionally.

She is married to her husband of forty-seven years and together they have three daughters, one son-in-law and two granddaughters—and a grand-dog.

CPSIA information can be obtained at www.ICGtesting.com
Printed in the USA
BVOW07s1424091113

335845BV00001B/2/P